The River

A Play

Charles Mander

A Samuel French Acting Edition

FOUNDED 1830

SAMUELFRENCH-LONDON.CO.UK
SAMUELFRENCH.COM

Copyright © 1979 by Charles Mander
All Rights Reserved

THE RIVER is fully protected under the copyright laws of the British Commonwealth, including Canada, the United States of America, and all other countries of the Copyright Union. All rights, including professional and amateur stage productions, recitation, lecturing, public reading, motion picture, radio broadcasting, television and the rights of translation into foreign languages are strictly reserved.

ISBN 978-0-573-02509-9

www.samuelfrench-london.co.uk

www.samuelfrench.com

FOR AMATEUR PRODUCTION ENQUIRIES

UNITED KINGDOM AND WORLD EXCLUDING NORTH AMERICA

plays@SamuelFrench-London.co.uk

020 7255 4302/01

Each title is subject to availability from Samuel French, depending upon country of performance.

CAUTION: Professional and amateur producers are hereby warned that *THE RIVER* is subject to a licensing fee. Publication of this play does not imply availability for performance. Both amateurs and professionals considering a production are strongly advised to apply to the appropriate agent before starting rehearsals, advertising, or booking a theatre. A licensing fee must be paid whether the title is presented for charity or gain and whether or not admission is charged.

The professional rights in this play are controlled by Samuel French Ltd, 52 Fitzroy Street, London, W1T 5JR.

No one shall make any changes in this title for the purpose of production. No part of this book may be reproduced, stored in a retrieval system, or transmitted in any form, by any means, now known or yet to be invented, including mechanical, electronic, photocopying, recording, videotaping, or otherwise, without the prior written permission of the publisher. No one shall upload this title, or part of this title, to any social media websites.

The right of Charles Mander to be identified as author of this work has been asserted by him in accordance with Section 77 of the Copyright, Designs and Patents Act 1988

THE RIVER

This play was specially commissioned for the Plymouth Theatre Company and was first presented at the Plymouth Arts Centre on 23rd November 1978 with the following cast:

Bert Thorne   Barry Woolgar

Richard   Cecil Humphreys

Tina, Richard's sister   Kathi Gordon

The play directed by Simon Dunmore
Setting by John Bell

The action takes place on part of the sea wall on the tidal estuary of a river in Somerset

Time: the present. An early morning in summer

SETTING

A ramshackle hut, a flimsy erection of corrugated iron and driftwood with a door and no windows, stands to the right of the stage. The door is partly open and bears the legend BEWARE OF DOG, handwritten in red paint. Below and to the left of the hut is a small, fragile, flat-bottomed fishing boat, known as a Flattener. The boat is pointed fore and aft, roughly constructed and lies upside down against the weather. It does not have to be very big or functional, but strong enough to be used as a seat from time to time.

This part of the sea wall is the base, and often the living quarters of a solitary salmon and eel fisherman. A once thriving occupation on the river, now virtually extinct. It is not a beautiful place and the river that sweeps on huge tides, unseen through the audience, is not beautiful either. It is a lonely, desolate, untidy jumble of fishing gear and flotsam, salmon traps made of willow, hand nets and cork floats mingle with discarded oil drums, plastic containers and all sorts of rubbish thrown up by the river. Some of the flotsam has been put to good use, oil drums serve as seats for instance, an old plank across two containers a useful bench against the hut. Human occupation has created some semblance of order, but on the whole, the fight against pollution on this part of the river has not been entirely successful.

But in spite of all this, there is an air of grandeur, a feeling of distance, a man could stay here all day and not meet another human being.

The scenery does not have to be substantial. The hut can be no more than a façade with a functional door, the boat little more than a suggestion. The play, however, would benefit from the use of rostrums to create the elevation and uneven structure of the river bank and sea wall and a cyclorama for a sense of space.

THE RIVER

The time is early morning on a summer day. The weather is fair

The stage is empty except for a boy's foot, a dirty canvas training boot and a bit of tattered blue jean protruding from the half open door of the hut. Gulls scream distantly a man whistles away off-stage and calls his dog

Man   Sandy? ... *(He whistles again)* Sandy?

The foot disappears

(Coming closer) Sandy? ... I'm telling you ! ... *(He whistles again)* Y'ere, boy ... y'ere. ... Damn thee eyes !

A weatherbeaten man in his fifties with a greying beard and ruddy complexion enters. He is scruffy and neglected looking, in old serge trousers, waders, a torn fisherman's jersey and an ancient yachting cap. He carries a pair of binoculars slung round his neck and is not in the best of moods. His name is Bert Thorne and he is probably the last of a generation of river fishermen. He goes to the edge of the bank and yells once more

Bert   Will thee come back y'ere. ... Bloody pie-eyed mongrel ! ... Sandy ! ... Sandy ! ... *(Muttering)* Damn and blast it ! *(He sits on an oil drum and peers across the river with his glasses. After a moment. Over his shoulder)* Come on out. *(He gets no response)* You heard l. ... Come on out !

A boy of about seventeen crawls out of the hut. He is an attractive, sensitive, rather immature lad, with the eyes of a dreamer. He has a slightly apologetic appearance that disguises the obstinacy and arrogance of adolescence. He is rumpled and exhausted, with the remains of a bruise on his cheek. His name is Richard. He wears faded, muddy jeans and a T shirt

Richard   *(hovering apologetically)* How did you know I was here?
Bert   *(still occupied with his glasses)* I'm not daft.
Richard   *(uncertainly)* How are things then? ... *(Bert says nothing)* ... *(Trying again)* You going on the river?
Bert   No.
Richard   Why's that then?
Bert   I 'aint got me dog.
Richard   Oh. ... *(After a moment)* Run off has he?

Bert	Likely.
Richard	Where's he to?
Bert	Dunno . . . didn't ask him.
Richard	*(after a while)* That's what I done.
Bert	*(without interest)* Eh?
Richard	Run off.
Bert	Oh ah.
Richard	Had a row with me dad.
Bert	*(thoughtfully)* Dog's randy . . . dips his wick.
Richard	I been on the river all night.
Bert	*(putting his glasses down and getting up)* Can't work with a randy dog. *(He looks at Richard for the first time)* You'll be hungered.
Richard	*(brightening)* Could do with a bite.
Bert	That figures. *(He goes into the hut)* . . . .
Richard	*(following him and speaking with more confidence)* Had a row with me dad.
Bert	I heard you . . . the first time. *(He emerges from the hut carrying an old canvas bag)*
Richard	Says I'm to go down the factory . . but I 'aint. *(Fiercely)* Not never I 'aint. . . . Never! *(Pause)* I got better things to do.
Bert	*(offering the boy a hunk of bread and cheese)* 'Ere. . . . You 'aint getting no more. 'Tis me breakfast.
Richard	Ta. *(He lays into the sandwich. After some moments with his mouth full)* Plashtic Bucketsh!
Bert	Eh?
Richard	*(swallowing energetically)* I shaid . . .
Bert	Don't speak with thee mouth full. *(He takes a huge bite himself)* Didn't thee mum ever tell 'ee that?
Richard	I said. . . . *(Completing the operation)* I said . . . plastic buckets! . . That's what I said.
Bert	Oh, ah. *(He picks his teeth)*
Richard	And if he thinks . . . if he thinks, I'm going down that grotty factory to make plastic buckets for the rest of me life. . . . He can piss in the wind!
Bert	Aw shut thee gob. *(He munches in gloomy silence)*
Richard	That's work for morons, that is. . . . I 'aint going and that's a fact.

   Bert does not reply. He is still munching morosely

   I run off . . . been on the river all night. *(Angrily)* Do you know *(He points to his bruise)* No I 'aint going down the factory . . . not never! Never! NEVER!

   Gulls clamour in the distance. Bert picks up his glasses

THE RIVER   7

Bert   (scanning the river) Them gulls is on to summat. Where's that bloody dog to? ... (He sweeps his glasses round, then returns and peers in the direction of the gulls) Booger it! 'Tis a salmon by there ... stranded. (Shouting) Sandy? ... SANDY! Where be to? (Giving up) What's he want to go running after bitches for, at his age?
Richard Going across?
Bert   No.
Richard Them gulls'll have that salmon.
Bert   Likely.
Richard You could go across in the boat.
Bert   No.
Richard Why not?
Bert   I 'aint got me dog.
Richard I'd help ... be yer mate.
Bert   (laughing) You?
Richard Yes, me! (He scowls at Bert) Why not? I been here often enough. ... Know the river....
Bert   Dog's edicated.
Richard (indignantly) So am I.... (Boastfully) Got an O level in history.
Bert   What's that got to do with fish?
Richard (casting round) Well ... I mean ... er....
Bert   Won't catch no fish with O levels ... for sure.
Richard (triumphantly) What about karate then?
Bert   Eh?
Richard Karate. (He makes a pass) I bet that dog can't do karate.
Bert   What's he want that for?
Richard Chopping the fish. (He leaps about) Ha! Hoy!
Bert   (watching him with a grin) Daft little booger. Always was a daft little booger. (He goes back to searching the river with his glasses) One of they collie bitches over to Strethun, I wouldn't be surprised. Randy as a toad.
Richard (subsiding) I should've chopped him ... used me karate ... give him summat to think about.... (He fingers his bruise) Bastard!
Bert   Shut thee gob ... yatter ... yatter....
Richard (indignantly) Well, 'tis my life 'aint it? ... mine! Not his. Go down the factory, he says ... get off yer backside ... do some honest work for once. And then he smashes me with the back of his hand, like I was ... like I was....
Bert   My old man smashed plenty of folk ... always at it he was. Didn't mean nowt. Put Johnny Lamb the milkman into hospital two days 'afore he snuffed it. Mind you there were a reason for that ... aye.... (He chuckles) There were a reason.
Richard An animal ... that's what he is ... an animal.

Bert	Powerful skittler however . . . spares, floppers, he were a good skittler.
Richard	Why should I do what he wants? Just 'cause he can't do nowt better himself? Day after day . . . going down that factory, turning out plastic buckets. . . .
Bert	'Course he didn't have no book learning. . . . No O levels . . . couldn't hardly write his name. But he were a damned good skittler. . . .
Richard	That's a living hell down there, a salt mine. Jesus . . . plastic buckets!
Bert	Bide quiet. . . . I'm thinking. . . .
Richard	I bet you could walk to Bristol on the plastic buckets, what my dad's turned out. And what's he got from them, eh? Nowt . . . bloody nowt!
Bert	Got a roof over his head.
Richard	Aye, a council roof . . . so what?
Bert	Got a car.
Richard	Oh yea . . . and a tele and a washing machine and a packet of flaming Fairy Liquid to go with it. If that's what life's about, then you can stuff it. I got better things to do.
Bert	Such as?
Richard	Working the river . . . like you.
Bert	Daft Booger . . . you'd not do that. *(He gets up and goes into the hut)*
Richard	*(gazing into the river)* I will . . . I will . . . I'll work the river.
	Bert returns with some salmon traps and starts to work on them
	Like you . . . like your Dad . . . and my Grandad . . . and all our folk 'afore us, like they done for more'n a thousand years. . . .
Bert	I hate that river.
Richard	Like in olden times . . . when King Arthur was around . . . and Sir Lancelot . . . and Sir Galahad . . . and all them knights. . . .
Bert	Treacherous, she is . . . I hate her.
Richard	*(dreaming)* And as I walked along the bank of the river, I saw a great stone, and it floated on top of the water. . . .
Bert	*(scowling at the river)* Bitch! Whore!
Richard	And into this stone was thrust a sword.
Bert	I hate that river! . . . *(He spits)*
Richard	King Arthur walked on these banks . . . must have . . . he's buried to Glastonbury . . . and Sir Galahad. . . . My heart is as the strength of ten, sang Sir Galahad gladly, because my heart is pure.
Bert	Killed my old man, she did. Sucked him up and spat him out twelve mile in the Channel. . . .

THE RIVER

Richard (*coming out of his reverie*) And do you know why he was pure of heart?
Bert Who?
Richard Sir Galahad. 'Cause he didn't have to go down no factory turning out plastic buckets and muck . . . (*he picks up a container*) . . . like this. Spewing out crap, wasting his life. And that's why I shan't never go down there . . . not never . . . (*He hurls the container off stage*) . . . NEVER!
Bert You've been off with they fairies again.
Richard What?
Bert They fairies—what you always on about—King Galahad—Sir Whatsisname—fairies.
Richard They 'aint fairies. How many times do I have to tell you?
Bert Fairies.
Richard They was real, they lived in these parts. Knights they was . . . on horses.
Bert (*enjoying himself*) Never.
Richard They fished the river, same as you.
Bert Not on horse they didn't.
Richard 'Course not! You thick or summat?
Bert Horses 'aint no bloody good for fishing. That's what thee needs . . . (*He points to the Flattener*) . . . a Flattener . . . and maybe a dog. Thee's got a screw missing son, that's for sure.
Richard I 'aint never! How can I have a screw missing? I've got an O level!
Bert Gor booger!! . . . 'Twas peaceful 'yere 'afore thee came. Go on home.
Richard I 'aint going home . . . not ever!
Bert Bide quiet then,
Richard (*muttering*) Always at you . . . always in your hair. When are you going to do this? . . . When are you going to do that? Go down the factory. . . . Get off your arse . . . layabout! . . . Yobo! . . . Drop out! (*He jumps up*) Sod 'em!! I 'aint never going home! I'm staying.
Bert Not 'yere thee 'aint.
Richard Why not?
Bert No fish.
Richard There's plenty of fish.
Bert Who says?
Richard I says.
Bert Oh, ah . . . an expert.
Richard Yes.
Bert On account of the O level, I daresay.
Richard Watch it! . . . I've got karate!

Bert	God save us! . . . I did forget!
	Richard scowls at Bert for a moment. Then his mood changes
Richard	Reckon I'll live here . . . on the bank. Sleep in the hut like you. We could work together. Make a great team, with my brains and your brawn. And when you've gone, I could take over, carry on the tradition.
Bert	Cheeky little booger!
Richard	Well, you'll not last forever . . . got to face facts.
Bert	*(chuckling)* Oh aye.
Richard	You 'aint got nobody, no progeny, no relatives. Except old Mrs Underwood up to Rose Cottage, and I can't see her fishing the river. Not with her bad feet.
Bert	I don't want nobody. I've got me dog.
Richard	He's on the way out for starters.
Bert	He bloody 'aint! Got plenty of vigour, go and ask they collie bitches.
Richard	*(hectoring)* Tottering he is . . . old and mangey. Oh, I know he's edicated, can swim the river and piss on the bad fish. But he's clapped out . . . half dead. . . .
Bert	*(wagging his finger)* Lay off me dog, boy! That's the best fishing dog in the County.
Richard	'Tis the only fishing dog in the County.
Bert	And there's plenty of life in him, plenty. He's just randy . . . that's his nature . . . can't help being randy . . . we're all randy.
Richard	*(giving Bert a funny look)* Aye . . . that's what they say . . . down the village.
Bert	What's that got to do with it?
Richard	Nowt. . . . *(With arrogance)* Well, I'm not like that. . . . I'm pure of heart.
Bert	You're three sheets to the wind!
Richard	*(after a moment—slyly)* Supposing summat's happened to that dog?
Bert	He's all right, he's just. . . .
Richard	*(quickly)* Supposing he's dead? . . . Supposing the milk lorry's had him, or the combine, or Birket's mower. . . .
Bert	*(getting to his feet in some agitation)* He's all right I tell thee . . . nowt's happened to he. . . .
Richard	He could be legless . . . chopped up by Birket's mower . . . a bleeding mass. . . .
Bert	Shut thee gob!
Richard	You'd be knackered without that dog. . . . You'd have to turn to me, 'cause I'm your only mate. The only one you got left. The only one that knows the river. You'd be knackered!

THE RIVER

Bert	Shut up! Or I'll fetch thee one!
Richard	I bet he's dead. I bet he won't piss on no more salmon, won't swim no more rivers....
Bert	I'm telling thee!...
Richard	Face facts! You know what they say about you down the village?
Bert	Don't 'ee go too far boy! Don't 'ee go too far!
Richard	*(rushing into disaster)* Loopy they call you, soft in the head. There's some would put you away ... shoot that old dog and put you away in a nut house ... they say you're evil, jump out at old ladies and such, and boys too, they say you have it off with sheep when there's....

Bert sends him sprawling with a blow from the back of his hand

	(Clutching his face) Not you?... Not you too? *(He buries his face in his hands)*
Bert	Shouldn't say.... 'Tis dirt ... dirt....
Richard	You didn't have to....
Bert	*(anguished)* I did son.... I did ... 'cause I 'aint got words. Nobody teached I, how to hurt with words.
Richard	*(writhing extravagantly)* Animal ... animal ... same as me dad.
Bert	Aye ... aye.... *(He shakes his head in misery, then goes to the bank and calls his dog)* Sandy?... Sandy?... Where be to boy?... come back 'yere ... come back ... come back....
Richard	*(getting to his feet and sensing Bert's distress)* Don't matter ... don't matter if you did smash me.... I'm used to it.
Bert	Go home son ... please go home.
Richard	But I love you, Mr. Thorne ... always have done ... since I were a nipper.
Bert	*(shaking his head)* Get on home ... leave I be.
Richard	I don't mind you hitting me ... if it makes you feel better.... I don't mind ... honest.

Bert stares out at the river

	'Twas only village talk.... 'Taint what I think.
Bert	Village talk ... muck! *(Calling)* Sandy?... where be to? Come back to I....
Richard	'Tis all muck down the village, 'cause they 'aint pure of heart. There's not many what's pure of heart these days. Not like in olden times, before them bloody factories came along, polluting things and such. A man could love, in them days ... like ... Sir Galahad, he loved King Arthur, and it wasn't muck. And if a man was real pure of heart, he could see wonderous things, like stones floating on water....
Bert	*(bleakly)* Stones don't float ... they sink.

Richard	Not in them days. Anything could happen in them days. And if a man were real pure like Sir Galahad, he could see a sword in that stone, and pull it out, and strike down evil . . . like . . . like . . . bloody plastics factories. . . .
Bert	Daft booger.
Richard	Reckon I might do that . . . if I see the stone floating along. I'd grab that sword . . . damn right I would. *(He sits dreaming for a moment or two)* He'll come back.
Bert	Reckon?
Richard	Aye . . . reckon.
Bert	'Course he will.
Richard	'Course.

They sit in silence for a time

Richard	But if he don't . . . what are you going to do?

Bert does not reply

	Now, if I was to be your mate. . . .
Bert	No.
Richard	Why not? . . . I'm as good as that old dog. I can piss on fish just as easy as him. I could swim the river too . . . easy. . . . 'Cause I'm tough. . . . *(He goes over to Bert and presents his arm and shoulder)* . . . Feel that . . . muscles like cannonballs.
Bert	*(uneasily)* Get off of I.
Richard	Feel 'em.
Bert	*(moving away)* NO!
Richard	*(grinning slyly)* What's the matter, Mr. Thorne?

Bert says nothing, only stares at the river with loathing

	(teasingly) Don't you want to feel my muscles?
Bert	*(swinging on him and speaking urgently)* Never try to swim that river . . . do thee hear . . . never!
Richard	Why not?
Bert	'Cause she'll have thee. Kill thee as easy as that! *(He snaps his fingers)*
Richard	Dog swims it.
Bert	Different . . . dog knows.
Richard	Can he swim on his back?
Bert	Eh?
Richard	Can he do butterfly? . . . Has he got a life-saving certificate? 'Cause I have.
Bert	Don't make no difference. She'll take thee . . . taken plenty 'afore . . . good strong swimmers . . . makes no difference to the river.
Richard	You scared of the river?
Bert	Oh aye . . . real scared.

THE RIVER 13

Richard : That's 'cause you 'aint pure of heart. If you was pure of heart, she wouldn't scare you. . . . She don't scare me.

Bert : *(looking at him—puzzled)* I don't reckon thee, boy. Gor booger it, there's time when I do think thee's soft in the head. Not in this 'ere world, up with they fairies. Goddamm it! Why do 'ee want to come by 'ere for in the first place? 'Tis. . . . *(He looks around)* 'Tis Godforsaken.

Richard : Godforsaken? . . . How can you say that? . . . 'Tis paradise.

Bert : Well, it may be your idea of paradise. . . . 'Taint mine. I don't see no paradise by 'ere. I don't see nowt but mud and muck. There 'aint hardly nowt can live up 'yere . . . nowt. . . . 'Cause of that there river, she's filthy and murderous and there's nowt can live in her. 'Taint paradise son . . . not up 'yere . . . 'tis desolation.

Richard : Don't talk like that. . . .

Bert : I hate that river . . . taken my whole life she has. Killed my old man and my brother Geoff, along with him, Flattener and all, just sucked 'em down. There's thirty foot in them tides, she'll turn a coaster when she has the mood. Twenty-five year ago she burst through this 'yere wall and took half the village . . . and now 'tis more than likely, she's taken my dog. *(He stares at the river with loathing)*

Richard : You're blind . . . blind! Can't see the truth of this river. . . . You're no better than the others.

Bert : There's nowt' yere for thee boy. Only a daft, fisherman, who 'aint got the sense to clear out, and that there river, and filth and muck and desolation. Why do 'ee come? . . . Why do 'ee come by 'ere. . . . 'Taint natural.

Richard : Blind . . . that's what you are . . . they have eyes and they see not.

Bert : There'll be no more fishing when I'm gone, that's for sure. River's dying . . . there's nowt can live in her. She's dying and there 'aint nothing up y'ere for the likes of thee.

Richard : *(wildly)* She 'aint dying! She 'aint! She's being murdered, murdered to death by that bloody factory! 'Tis our river . . . ours . . . and those bastards up there are killing her! Christ! *(He rushes down to the bank)* If only I could get my hands on that bloody sword!

Bert : There 'aint no sword. Get down, get out of the clouds.

Richard : You don't understand . . . you're ignorant!

Bert : *(laughing)* I am that. For if I weren't, I'd have gone off with the others . . . down the factory . . . got myself a place to live . . . a family . . . kids . . . maybe a car. *(Bitterly)* There 'aint no sword, and there 'aint no stone floating on the water. 'Tis all dreams.

Richard : *(turning on him)* You traitor . . . you filthy traitor. I loved you . . . like King Arthur you was to me, a light shining in the wilderness . . . God, you're pathetic . . . no better than them . . . full of evil faith . . . and . . . and poor belief. . . .

Bert	Dreams . . dreams . . . put your feet on the earth boy . . . grow up.
Richard	*(furiously)* Jump in the bloody river!

Richard stalks out in a fury

Bert	*(calling anxiously after him)* Where be to?
Richard	*(off)* Get stuffed!
Bert	Don't do nothing daft! . . . Do you hear I? . . . don't do nothing daft! *(Getting no response)* Damn and blast it! *(He goes back to his traps. After a moment he gets up and goes to the river's edge—calls)* Sandy? . . . Sandy? . . . 'Yere, boy . . . 'yere.

Richard rushes in and makes for the hut

Richard	*(scrambling into the hut)* I'm not here. . . .
Bert	What?
Richard	If she asks where I am. I'm not here. . . . I'm dead . . . or summat. . . .
Bert	Who?
Richard	Our Tina . . . she's coming up the wall. . . . What's she playing at? . . . Stupid cow.
Tina *(off)*	Hoy . . . I saw yer.
Richard	Oh God! I'm not here. . . *(He hides in the hut)* I've drownded myself!
Bert	*(shrugging)* Daft booger.

He goes back to his work and after a moment or two Tina enters. She is not the sort of girl one is likely to meet on the river at seven o'clock in the morning. Or indeed at any time. She is an office girl, with an office pallor and apart from an outsized pair of gumboots she is dressed for the office. She is Richard's sister, about eighteen years of age with pallid, rather self-conscious, good looks and sexuality. She is not at her best, being livid and worn out by the long walk. She approaches Bert with some trepidation, well aware of his reputation in the village and half hoping that he might do something outrageous.

Tina	*(feigning surprise)* Oh? . . er . . . Hi.
Bert	Fine day.
Tina	Pardon?
Bert	'Tis a fine day . . . no good for fishing, however.
Tina	Oh. *(She giggles nervously)*

Bert winks at her and gestures towards the hut.

Tina	*(springing back—alarmed)* What?
Bert	*(winking and gesturing—then speaking loudly)* Reckon I'll go behind the hedge.
Tina	Oh . . . er. . . .

THE RIVER

Bert   What goes in must come out. . . . *(He starts to go. Then stops)* You seen a dog?
Tina   Pardon?
Bert   Kind of collie-dog with cross eyes.
Tina   *(nervously)* Er . . . no.
Bert   Run off he has . . . 'cause he's randy. *(He winks again and gestures towards the hut)* . . . morning.

>He strolls out
>Tina watches him go, with her mouth open. Then her rage returns and she clumps over to the hut

Tina   Come out you little shit! *(She gets no answer)* Are you coming out, Richard? . . . or do I have to pull you out by your ears?
Richard   *(emerging)* What you doing up here, Tina?
Tina   God! I could kill you! I could wring your bloody neck! What you bloody well playing at?
Richard   *(picking up a salmon trap and inspecting it casually)* Nowt . . none of your business.
Tina   *(furiously)* You know what you done? You have any idea what's been happening since you buggered off?
Richard   Nope . . . and I don't care.
Tina   You don't care? . . . God! You're a right little shit! They've gone spare! Mum's been climbing up the wall! Dad's been feeding her Valium like Maltesers. Up and down, in and out of the toilet, all bloody night—banging the door. Not had a wink of sleep . . . and I need eight hours. God! I could murder you! God, my feet are killing me. *(She collapses on to a drum and takes her boots off)* God!
Richard   *(examining the trap with studied indifference)* I 'aint going back.
Tina   *(massaging her feet)* Oh, be your age.
Richard   I am being my age. I 'aint going back, so you can piss off!
Tina   *(bridling)* Don't you talk to me like that! 'Aint you got no sense of responsibility?
Richard   I'm leading my own life from now on. I'm staying here.
Tina   *(nodding off stage)* With him?
Richard   Why not?
Tina   *(narrowing her eyes)* What you been up to?
Richard   None of your business.
Tina   *(in a loud whisper)* You know he's a freak?
Richard   Crap. . . .
Tina   He is! You should see the way he looked at me. . . . *(She shivers pleasantly)*
Richard   He don't fancy you, Tina. . . . He's got more sense. *(He looks away across the river glumly)* Dog's the only thing what he fancies.

Tina	Among other things.... *(She makes a face)* ... From what I hear. So you'd best watch your back.
Richard	Village talk ... muck!
Tina	*(putting her boots on)* Coming then?
Richard	No.
Tina	*(indignantly)* Look, shit-face! I been sent up here at God knows what hour in the morning, without any breakfast, and damn-all sleep to bring you back. Mum and Dad are climbing up the wall. Don't you understand?
Richard	I 'aint going back. I 'aint going down that sodding factory.
Tina	Where else can you go, with what you got? ... One O level ... in History.... *(She laughs)* ... I mean nobody's going to take you on because of your scintillating personality are they? ... You're going down that factory and that's that!
Richard	*(obstinately)* I bloody 'aint. I'm not going.
Tina	Okay ... if you want to be a freak.... *(She nods off)* ... Like him.
Richard	*(shouting)* He's not a freak!
Tina	Keep your voice down, for God's sake.... He'll hear.
Richard	He's my mate.
Tina	Oh yea?.... *(She grins knowingly. She looks at her watch)* God! Look at the time. If I'm late for work ... I'll kill you. *(She gets up)* You coming or not?
Richard	I'm staying.
Tina	Don't be thick.
Richard	I tell you, I'm staying. Now piss off!
Tina	They'll have the police on you.
Richard	So what!
Tina	He's a freak, you know. A nutter. They'll have the police on you, and him too ... more than likely.
Richard	You'll be late for work, Tina.
Tina	*(indignantly)* God you're a selfish little prick! Don't you never think of nobody but yourself?
Richard	No ... 'cause nobody thinks of me!
Tina	Oh ... you poor sod. What you think they sent me up here for? To pick mushrooms or summat? Grow up!
Richard	Leave me alone.
Tina	What's so wrong with the factory? Tell me that? What's so wrong with it?
Richard	You wouldn't understand ... you're one of them.
Tina	*(dangerously)* One of what?
Richard	*(vaguely)* Them.... Look, hadn't you better get on down there?
Tina	What am I going to tell Mum and Dad?
Richard	I don't know ... tell 'em I've gone to Glastonbury ... joined the hippies ... that I've gone mad on magic mushrooms and thrown

THE RIVER

	myself into the tumultuous river . . . make summat up . . . you're good at that. Only leave me alone—I've work to do.
Tina	Work? . . . Work? . . . You call this . . . work?
Richard	Aye . . . work . . . 'cause that's what we was made for. Tilling the soil . . . fishing the river . . . going free. Not wasting our lives down some bloody factory . . . banging a typewriter and having it off with the chargehand in the tea break.
Tina	You mind what you're saying, Richard I . . . you mind your tongue.
Richard	Well, it's true, 'aint it?
Tina	*(furiously)* If I had the time. . . . If I had. . . .
Richard	But you 'aint . . . 'cause you got to go off at nine o'clock with all them other zombies and lay your eggs in bloody rows like battery hens. Cluck. . . . Cluck . . . bloody cluck . . . cluck. . . .
Tina	Do you know what I'd do if I were them? . . .
Richard	Cluck . . . cluck. . . . .
Tina	I'd exterminate you. . . . I'd put you down!
Richard	*(infuriatingly)* Keep your voice down, Tina . . . he'll hear you. Cluck . . . cluck. . . .
Tina	*(lowering her voice)* There's too many of your sort about. Freaking out. Living off handouts. Sponging off the workers. You're a loafing little shit! That's what you are. . . . Yes. . . . *(She clumps off)* I'd put you down. . . .
Richard	Cluck . . . cluck. . . .
Tina	And don't you bloody cluck at me! You'll be clucking on the other side of your face when Dad hears about this. . . . Cheerio. . . .
	Tina goes
Richard	*(shouting after her)* Get stuffed . . . sex mad cow!
Tina	*(off)* Freak!
	Richard kicks the ground petulantly. Bert returns
Richard	*(still fuming)* Cow!
	Bert looks at him, but says nothing
	What she want to come up here for? . . . Stupid cow.
Bert	Got more sense than what thee has. . . .
Richard	You was listening then?
Bert	Likely.
Richard	More'n likely!
Bert	No sense . . . should've gone with her.
Richard	*(suddenly turning on him—angrily)* Do I stink or summat?
Bert	Eh?
Richard	Why do you keep trying to see me off?
Bert	Just talking sense.
Richard	Christ, you're as bad as they are. Why should I go with that cow?

	Don't owe her nowt . . . don't owe none of them nowt. Didn't ask to be born.
Bert	Neither did I, son, but I'm 'yere.
Richard	Three pints of scrumpy and a quick screw, that's how I come into the world. A bloody inconvenience. . . .
Bert	Ah, shut thee gob!
Richard	That's all you can say, isn't it? . . . "Shut thee gob!" . . . "Go on home!" You're like a bloody parrot, you are!

He sits down and starts to take off his boots

Bert	Hoy! What's on?
Richard	None of your business.
Bert	*(getting angry)* I asked civil . . . now answer civil!
Richard	*(ripping off his shirt)* Going to smash me again are you? . . . Take your hand to me? . . . You don't give a shit what I do! You're no better than the others . . . don't give a shit! *(He starts to remove his trousers)* Fancy me do you? . . . Like this?
Bert	*(shouting)* Get they things back on. . . .
Richard	Or do you fancy our Tina? . . . Hell, I bet you seen more through them glasses than just fish. . . .
Bert	Get they things on, boy! 'Afore I. . . .
Richard	'Afore you what, Mr. Thorne? . . . 'afore you what?
Bert	*(clenching his fists)* Get they clothes on! What's got into thee?
Richard	Just going for a swim, Mr. Thorne . . . nowt wrong with that.
Bert	Thee bloody 'aint!
Richard	Oh yes I am . . . I'm going to swim that river. See what's left of that salmon.
Bert	*(getting in front of Richard)* Oh no, son . . . that thee 'aint.
Richard	I'm not scared. River don't scare me. If that dog can swim her . . . so can I. *(He dodges round Bert and makes for the bank)*
Bert	Come back 'yere—daft bugger . . . she'll kill 'ee. . . . She'll suck 'ee down!
Richard	No . . . she'll not do that . . . 'cause I'm pure of heart. . . .
Bert	*(shouting at Richard—very agitatedly)* What's got into thee? . . . Bloody little vool! Come back 'yere!
Richard	*(taking up a diving position—fantasizing)* And I saw a great stone, and she was floating on the water and I have the strength of ten because my heart is pure and I 'aint scared.
Bert	*(hurling himself after Richard)* Stop it! . . . Stop it! . . . Wake up! Wake up you daft vool. . . . For Christ sakes wake up!

Bert grabs Richard as he is about to dive and brings him to the ground

Richard	*(thrashing about furiously)* Let go of me! Let go! . . . What do you care? . . . What do you bloody well care?

THE RIVER

Bert	I care, boy. ... I do! ... Now bide quiet!
Richard	*(yelling and fighting)* No you don't! You don't! Give more thought to that bloody dog than you do to me! Let go!
Bert	*(forcing him down)* Thee 'aint going in that river... If'n I do have to knock thee bloody head off!
Richard	Lay off will yer! ... What does it matter if I drown myself? Who'd bloody care. ... I don't mean nowt to nobody. ... I'm just a dirty thought ... shat out to make plastic buckets! ... A bloody inconvenience... what does it matter? ... *(He subsides—exhausted from his efforts)* ... What does it matter? ... What does it matter?
Bert	*(standing over him, and throwing down his clothes)* Put 'em back on! ... 'Taint seemly!
Richard	*(making one last defiant gesture)* Freak! ... Kinky old freak!

Bert raises his fists

All right! All right! ... Don't do yourself an injury. *(He starts to get dressed)*

Bert	More like it. ... That's sense. *(Watching Richard closely)* Now then. ... What's the game?
Richard	No game. ... 'Taint no game.
Bert	Oh ah. ...
Richard	*(sullenly)* You wouldn't understand.
Bert	*(with some anger)* Now listen 'yere! I 'aint daft! I know what thee has in mind and I don't like it, 'cause I do care for thee, boy.
Richard	That's a joke!
Bert	No. 'Taint. 'Taint no joke. *(He moves away, full of frustration at the inadequacy of his vocabulary)* ... Blast it!
Richard	'Tis a joke ... but it 'aint funny.
Bert	*(turning)* Now harken to I. ...
Richard	Why should I? Why should. ...
Bert	*(his voice powerful with ferocity)* Harken! I did say! ...

Richard subsides

Now, I'm a lonely man and I 'aint got words. But I care for thee, boy, always have done, since 'ee first come up 'yere as a nipper, with thee head full of fancies, and fairy tales, and daft ways and such. Made I laugh thee did ... and that's powerful good for a man. Thee and that old dog ... just about all I do have for myself ... after ... more'n fifty year ... and that's the truth.

Richard	Reckon?
Bert	Aye ... reckon.
Richard	Then why see me off? Why treat me like I was shit ... if you care for me?
Bert	I don't never do that son ... never. ... Thee'll not say I do that.
Richard	Then why can't I be your mate?

Bert	Things change . . . they change . . . and 'taint no good pretending they don't.
Richard	*(dogmatically)* I 'aint going down that factory.
Bert	That factory. . . . *(He laughs)* I'll tell 'ee summat . . . you'll maybe not reckon it . . . for thee's too full of shouting and yelling and cussing to listen to sense. But I'll tell 'ee. When I were your age . . . maybe a bit younger, that there factory were just starting up. Making bricks, she was. 'Twere like the second coming in these 'yere parts. Good money . . . regular work. Never had that 'afore see . . . not by 'ere. That's where I did want to bide . . . and all they young folk. . . . There's many would've selled their souls for a job up there. . . . *(He nods towards the factory)*
Richard	Never! Never!
Bert	Oh aye! . . . A man could eat regular up there, have shoes on his feet and maybe a cycle. That were living . . . that were life . . . that's where I did want to bide.
Richard	Then why didn't you? . . . If you loved the bloody place so much . . . why didn't you bide there?
Bert	'Cause of my old man. He wouldn't have it see. He'd fished the river and his dad afore he, and his dad afore that, and way back. Never done nowt else, there weren't nowt else. So I had to fish the river too, 'cause he said so, and I did never have the guts to stand against him. *(He sits, shaking his head)* Funny 'aint it? . . . 'Cause with thee. . . . 'Tis arse about tit.
Richard	Well, 'tis better up here, than down a bloody factory.
Bert	Reckon?
Richard	Well, of course it is. . . . Christ, I know.
Bert	Do 'ee?
Richard	For sure.
Bert	Ah . . . same as 'ee know, 'ee can swim that river, eh?
Richard	'Course.
Bert	*(getting up)* I'll show 'ee summat. *(He goes down to the river's edge and looks upstream)* Aye, that'll do . . . see it? *(He points out across the river)*
Richard	What?
Bert	That there . . . see her? . . . that there galvanised oil drum, coming by on the tide. . . .
Richard	Oh aye . . . what's so bloody strange about that? . . . Ten a penny they are.
Bert	You just watch her . . . over to Black Rock . . . go on watch her.
Richard	'Aint you got nothing better to do?
Bert	Watch her, I said.
Richard	Well, okay . . . I am.
Bert	Don't 'ee take your eyes off her.

They watch her carefully for a moment

THE RIVER

Richard	I don't know what you're trying to prove, I reckon you've gone soft in the head. I mean....
Bert	*(triumphantly)* There!
Richard	Jesus!... *(He whistles)*
Bert	Down current... 'tis the tide... that's a whirlpool. You'll not see that drum, 'afore Steart Island, three mile off.
Richard	What about the dog then?
Bert	Edicated... he don't swim when the tide's like that.
Richard	*(moving to the Flattener and sitting)* Maybe... maybe.... Maybe, I'll get on one of they coasters up to Dunball. Sign on... sail to foregn parts... like... like Barry Island... or Swansea.... Make my fortune... go down a coal mine... better than the plastics factory, I mean anything's better than that... even a coal mine or is it?
Bert	That old dog's been gone a sight too long... a sight too long.
Richard	Surely... there must be... I mean... I mean....
Bert	Sandy?... Sandy?... where be to?... Come on home, boy... come on home. Saandy!... Saandy!... Saandy!
Richard	*(suddenly leaping up with excitement)* 'Tis there! 'Tis there!
Bert	*(startled)* Gor booger I.... Can't 'ee keep quiet for two minutes?
Richard	'Tis the sword!... The sword... there... thrust into a stone, floating on the water. Can't you see her? Flashing in the sunlight ... by there... by there....
Bert	Calm down will 'ee... mad booger!...
Richard	Can't you see her?... Can't you see her flashing on the water?
Bert	I can't see nowt... bide quiet will 'ee!
Richard	No, you wouldn't... you wouldn't. Folk like you don't see nothing... can't hardly see your feet. Give us them! *(He snatches the glasses from Bert)*
Bert	Hoy!
Richard	That sword's special... shining and sparkling and wonderous... she's special... just special... just... just.... *(He thrusts the glasses back at Bert and turns his back on the river)* Oh shit!... SHIT!
Bert	Aye, there's plenty of that in the river. *(He peers through the glasses)*
Richard	*(castigating himself)* Fool! Daft bloody fool!... Berk!
Bert	Ah, I got her now.... Could've fooled I.... Would 'ee reckon it. *(He chuckles sympathetically)*
Richard	Go on, laugh... laugh.... 'Tis only a bloody nit, would see summat wonderous in bloody rubbish.
Bert	Oh.... I wouldn't say that, boy. 'Tis a packing case with tin foil... and with the sun on her, flashing like.... *(He re-adjusts his glasses)* Well, damn me eyes!... *(He takes out an old rag from his pocket and cleans the lenses, his face animated with suppressed excitement)*

Richard	I should've known. . . . Jesus Christ, I should've known. . . . 'Tis always the same. Whenever you look for summat wonderous, turns out muck . . . just muck! 'Tis always the same . . . sod it! Bloody sod it! *(He buries his head in his hands)*
Bert	By God! . . . *(He peers intently through his glasses)* 'Taint so. . . . No, by God, 'taint so. *(He puts his glasses down and moves purposefully to the hut)* Come on, boy . . . lend a hand. *(He disappears into the hut)*
Richard	Lend a hand? . . . what for?
Bert	The dog, boy . . . the dog . . . didn't thee see him?
Richard	No.
Bert	*(in the hut)* Well, he's there. *(He comes to the door and shouts across the river)* Stay there, Sandy, boy . . . don't 'ee try nothing daft now . . . w're coming for 'ee.
Richard	Where is he? . . . I never saw no dog . . . never saw him.
Bert	*(coming out of the hut, with his arms full of boots and gear)* No, thee wouldn't. 'Cause thee was too taken up looking for they swords and stones floating on the water and such. But he were there . . . right behind that old packing case, up to his belly in mud, with the tide about him. *(He laughs)* He'll not be so keen to dip his wick after this. *(Shouting)* Stay there you randy bastard! . . . We're coming after 'ee! *(To Richard)* Well? . . . going to lend a hand? . . . or sit on thee arse all day?
Richard	*(getting up slowly, casually)* Reckon I might . . . reckon you'll need me.
Bert	*(looking at him with a twinkle)* Aye . . . reckon.
Richard	Okay then . . . let's go. *(They start to go. But Richard stops and shouts at the dog)* Hoy, Sandy! . . . you clapped out old rat bag! Do you hear me? . . . Jump in the river . . . jump in the river and drown thee bloody self!
Bert	*(severely. Wagging his finger at Richard)* Hoy. . . . Now then! *(But Richard is grinning innocently and Bert's mood changes)* Naw! Got more sense . . . he'll not jump in the river . . . the dog'll not do that. . . . Dog's got more sense.
	They look at each other for a moment or two grinning Reckon?
Richard	*(still grinning)* Get lost!
	Bert slaps him on the back and they hurry off
Bert	*(as he goes, shouting to the dog)* All right me old son . . . we're coming . . . we're coming. . . .
	They go out and the play ends

www.ingramcontent.com/pod-product-compliance
Ingram Content Group UK Ltd.
Pitfield, Milton Keynes, MK11 3LW, UK
UKHW061016220426
5322IPUK00032B/556